Spiritual Encounter with the Shroud

Caspar McCloud

Interviews

with L.A. Marzulli

by Caspar McCloud

Spiritual Encounter with the Shroud
Caspar McCloud Interviews with L.A. Marzulli

May 2015 - Updated
January 2015

Transcribed Interview
with Caspar McCloud and L. A. Marzulli

Published by:

Life Application Ministries, Inc.
P.O. Box 165 Mt. Aukum, CA 95656
truthfrees@lifeapplicationministries.org

www.lifeapplicationministries.org

Permission is granted to use this material for teaching and ministry purposes only.
Please do not reproduce or sell for profit.

Cover Picture:

© 1978 Barrie M. Schwortz Collection, STERA, Inc. All Rights Reserved.

Back Cover Photo "Paid in Full": Karen Jacks

Russ Breault, President, Shroud of Turin Education Project, Inc. (www.ShroudEncounter.com)

Barrie Schwortz - Edited

Printer: createspace.com

INDEX

Endorsements 4
Preface 7

Questions

1. What got you interested in the Shroud of Turin? 8
2. Why do you believe this is the real
   burial cloth of Jesus? 8
3. What is your take on the Carbon 14 dating,
   the results of which has been held up by
   skeptics that the Shroud is a 14
   Century forgery? 12
4. Why should Christians care about the Shroud? 14
5. How do you think the image was made? 14
6. The nail prints are not found in the area of the
   hand in what is depicted in most works of art.
   Why is that? 17
7. How do you think the image was put on
   the cloth? 18
8. What would you say to the skeptic? 20
9. Are you familiar with the so-called restoration
   done on the Shroud and how it destroyed any
   forensic evidence for future generations? 23
10. Your closing thoughts. 24

Final Thoughts 30

Pictures 35

Salvation Prayer 46

More Books and Teachings 47

Contact Us 48

ENDORSEMENTS

I am pleased to know Caspar McCloud as a true man of God. He died and came back to life with a new heart. I have never met anyone more sold out to the cause of Christ than Caspar. In 1978 he saw an image of the Shroud and was so moved by its powerful witness he was born again and later inspired to write a magnificent song about his experience. Caspar and I have ministered together several times. I know you will be moved by the Scriptural and Spiritual truth imparted by Caspar in this book. Read and be blessed!

Russ Breault, President,
Shroud of Turin Education Project, Inc.
(www.ShroudEncounter.com)

Caspar speaks to us passionately and from his heart and takes us beyond the science to share the powerful, spiritual message of the Shroud of Turin with his readers....

Barrie Schwortz
Shroud of Turin Research Project (STURP)

I was blessed and delighted to meet a brother in Christ Caspar McCloud who sent me and my wife many of his books absolutely FREE. When I could see and read his amazing God given talents in writing many books. I asked him to join me in witting our popular Shroud booklet: The Shroud of Turin Speaks for Itself [Paperback] which Climbed to #1 - out of 1,047 results on Amazon.com. Caspar McCloud and I had much in common with the tangible, unmistakable, unconcealed, undisguised, distinct, distinguishable, prominent, striking, evidence of the Father God's yearning love visible for all to see, comprehend and gain faith, all locked for 2000 years and revelled like a fossil in a time capsule.

Even today we never fail to see the visible, observable, noticeable, "easily seen blatantly glaring love of God" and His son's crucifixion, death, and the ultimate Resurrection of Jesus (Yeshua) meaning Salvation. All on the Shroud of Turin and the Sudarium of Oviedo.

Simon Brown
Realdiscoveries.org

I have been fascinated by the Shroud of Turin for over 34 years now. I have studied it and believe it is the burial cloth of our Risen Savior, Yashua/Jesus. I have come to call it Gods Calling Card.

When you dive into the interview with Pastor Caspar McCloud, you will find yourself learning about the most probed, studied artifact on planet earth. Caspar will guide you through the vast information about the Shroud and his comments are both enlightening and erudite!

L. A. Marzulli
Author, Researcher, Lecturer,
Host of the Watchers Series
www.lamarzulli.net
www.lamarzulli.wordpress.com

There are few artifacts more undeniably enigmatic than the Shroud of Turin. As Dame Isabel Piczek told us a few year ago, "it was an event horizon" in trying to describe the true nature of how earth-shattering the moment was that created, what scientists later discovered, a 3D image on the Shroud. Caspar McCloud has embraced the topic and has put together a booklet that answers some of the questions about the Shroud and what it might mean. There are only a few people, (I could count on one hand) that I've met with what I would call a "pastor's heart" like Caspar has. He is not only interested in the Shroud phenomena, but he deeply cares about others and will pray for you at the drop of a hat, which he has done for me many times—always with my respect and appreciation. Prayers like that are becoming rarer these days. He also has an unusual talent for music and has played with some of the best of them, so this booklet is coming from a musical, loving and caring individual that is really impressed with the essence of what the Shroud means—perhaps our only physical evidence remaining that Jesus Christ could have existed, and what we believe might also be the most important evidence of all—His resurrection. You decide.

Richard Shaw
Director of "The Watchers" and
"The Bible Codes"

Note to Reader:

As with most writings or conversations one engages in, it seems to me there are always new thoughts, information and ideas you would like to go back and add in. Fortunately, as the author I am able to do so now and have added some lines of information in a few places for clarification.

I recall, as a young art student, learning how Leonardo Da Vinci felt when he never finished a single one of his masterpieces. It's clear we are all a work in progress this side of Heaven, I dare say, with an enigmatic smile.

Philippians 1:6,*"Being confident of this very thing, that he which hath begun a good work in you will perform it until the day of Jesus Christ:"*

PREFACE

It seems most people I ask no matter where I travel to do not know much about the Shroud of Turin. Many have not even ever heard about it, although some may have a vague recollection about hearing something about a ancient cloth with the picture of Jesus on it. Over the years I have found sharing the information that I have researched and collected about the Shroud of Turin has helped lead many to come to an understanding and acceptance of Christ's amazing offer of salvation which includes healing miracles for today.

Hebrews 13:8, *"Jesus Christ the same yesterday, and to day, and for ever."*

The idea for this booklet came from an interview I did with my friend L. A. Marzulli in 2013 that was published in his PP&S magazine. Politics, Prophesy and the Supernatural for which I am also a staff writer. After co writing, "The Shroud of Turin Speaks For Itself', with Simon Brown in UK, the Lord arranged for me to meet and work with one of the foremost experts on the Shroud of Turin today—Russ Breault. If you ever have an opportunity to experience a presentation with Marzulli in person or with Breault's Shroud Encounter, I encourage you in the strongest terms possible to attend their meetings and be blessed by these servants of the Lord.

In the meantime I pray this booklet will help you understand the importance of establishing in your own hearts the question of whether or not the Shroud of Turin is the actual burial cloth of Jesus Christ of Nazareth, Messiah Yeshua and what that means for you today. More importantly, I pray this helps answer the question of the vital message we are presented with which is supernaturally recorded on the Shroud.

In Christ's love,
Caspar McCloud
Pastor - Upper Room Fellowship

THE INTERVIEW

Join us as we embark on this amazing interview that reveals the details of the Shroud of Turin. Dr. L. A. Marzulli interviewed Pastor Caspar McCloud asking the following questions:

1. What got you interested in the Shroud of Turin?

Back in the 70's as a teenager my friend, mentor and fellow musician Phil Keaggy, started sharing the Gospel with me. At that time I was also pursuing a career as an Artist, growing up admiring Da Vinci and the paintings of the Per-Raphaelites which naturally attracted me to the intellectual side of things. Soon after Phil started trying to win me to Christ, a fellow Art student showed me a poster of the Shroud, which had a very profound effect on me when I realised what I was actually looking at. I recall shortly thereafter I came across an article about the Shroud of Turin, and I was totally convinced the Shroud was genuine after seeing the evidence. It was only a matter of a few days after this before events and things were orchestrated in my life that caused me to totally surrender my life to Christ. I was overwhelmed with the truth of the Gospel and understanding that the Shroud was genuine certainly played a major role in this.

2. Why do you believe this is the real burial cloth of Jesus?

Personally it appears to me that the evidence is rather overwhelming that this indeed is the burial cloth of Christ. The Lord gave us an amazing supernatural holographic type picture which has preserved a moment of Jesus Christ of Nazareth's glorious resurrection. Let's start with the fact that Pete Shumacher, who was the technician of the NASA VP-8 Image Analyzer, helped discover that the Shroud actually is a 3D topographical image, which shows very clearly the image of a man in three dimensions, showing that the cloth had been wrapped around a real person. Might I add that means the Shroud truly is extraordinary, and no one in this world is able to duplicate this. It is supernatural and with all the advances of modern technology and even if we were able to clearly understand how it was produced we still not be able to recreate this phenomena. The evidence clearly tells us that the distance imaging information collected was supernaturally encoded within the image on the Shroud at its formation. This alone virtually guarantees to the world that the image on the Shroud was caused by Christ's resurrection and is not a painting of any sort at all. It is also the only two dimensional image in our world that displays this amazing three dimensional property.

The more one studies the evidence of the Shroud, the more absurd the theory that some medieval genius created it becomes. If you could collect and gather the brightest minds in science today, all the modern day Da Vinci's and Einstein's and ask them to create some sort of image using advanced technology that would not be available until 500 years later, how could they even begin to embark on such a task? Just to put things in proper perspective here.

The image on the Shroud of Turin is probably one of the most analyzed subjects in this world because it reveals the torture that Jesus/Yashua suffered with the forty lashes, there are actually about 120 scourge marks on the body, front and back consistent from a Roman three-thonged whip which had metal bits at the end which tore and ripped at the flesh. You can clearly see the scars and His pierced body, along with the puncture wounds from the crown of thorns which pierced His head on the Shroud. It also shows us His plucked out beard and records the humiliation He endured by the Romans, who punched him in the face causing Jesus—the Saviour of the world—swollen cheekbones which are evident on the image.

The Shroud also shows us the damaged knee with dirt particles from falling whilst carrying his own cross. It shows us the excruciating agony he suffered from the blood on his body and blood shed from his pierced hands and feet, it is a silent witness to the absolute horror of the cross of crucifixion. The shroud shows the mark made by the spear wound in Jesus's side that convinced the Romans soldiers that he was indeed completely dead before they removed him off that cross, fulfilling the ancient prophecy, and making it unnecessary to break his legs to speed up the dying process. According to tradition, they needed to take him off the cross before the Sabbath began in order to satisfy the religious leaders.

The Shroud also records the ultimate supernatural triumph of the Resurrection of Jesus Christ of Nazareth which brings us Salvation today for all who believe and accept Him as the sacrificial Lamb of God, as their personal Saviour. There is only one way to be saved for all eternity and it is personal between you and the Lord Messiah Yashua/Jesus Christ of Nazareth.

The Lord provided all this as evidence to be recorded supernaturally on the Shroud of Turin that the world might believe, not to mention all the other supernatural signs and wonders and healing miracles and testimonies that have continued since Messiah Jesus/Yashua sent the Holy Spirit to Baptize and empower His true disciples in every proceeding generation (John 14:12).

Scientists have also now believed that they have confirmed numbers of herbs and microscopic grains of pollen on the Shroud from dozens of species of plants that are known to only grow in Israel and around Jerusalem, proving it be of an Israeli origin. There is much more compelling evidence, for example, a number of scientists also believe that there are in fact two ancient Palestinian coins discovered that appear to be covering the eyes of the image on the Shroud, minted by Pontius Pilate in AD 30 and

31. These are extremely rare coins and it appears there are only about five known to exist today in this world. However, because of the coarse weave of the cloth it is one of those places where it is rather difficult identifying the inscriptions with absolute precision at this time.

Then, there is the fact that the Romans, apparently to spare the family and friends further trauma, in an ironic act of courtesy covered the face of Jesus with a Napkin whilst taking him off the cross. This napkin is called the Sudarium of Oviedo: There is no image on this cloth, however the blood stains match perfectly with the image on the Shroud of Turin. History also recorded the whereabouts of the Sudarium of Oviedo which helps prove that the Shroud of Turin is in fact genuine.

The Bible tells us that when the disciples, John and Peter, ran to investigate the now empty tomb of the resurrected Jesus, Simon Peter who had been running a bit behind John, went right past him and into the tomb and saw the linen burial cloth lying there. Along with the face cloth that had covered Jesus' face, the Bible says and he saw, and believed. (John 20:4-8) What was it they saw that absolutely convinced them that indeed Jesus had been resurrected?

The Apostles, John and Peter, must have seen straightaway the burial wrappings and something absolutely convinced them that no one had stolen the body of Jesus. My best educated Holy Spirit guess here is that all circumstances told that they immediately understood the profound significant historical moment here seeing the burial Shroud. It was left exactly the way it had been wrapped when they had left the dead body of Jesus 3 days before. Only now the body was missing. Perhaps it now looked sort of like an empty collapsed cocoon? Did they understand that if someone had stolen the body they would have taken the burial shroud as well? Was it that no one had unwound the strips of sticky-spice drenched cloth that tied the whole Shroud to keep it on the body? Or was it that they opened the Shroud and saw the evidence of the recorded miracle of the image of Christ? The Bible tells us in Proverbs 25:2 *"It is the glory of God to conceal a thing: but the honour of kings is to search out a matter."*

In these last days, I believe the image of the Shroud is still telling us of the incredible love the Lord Jesus has for each one of us. I pray it causes everyone to make their peace with God before they leave this world, in Jesus Yashua's name.

3. What is your take on the Carbon 14 dating, the results of which has been held up by skeptics that the Shroud is a 14 century forgery?

First off, all the scientists who interpreted the findings of the 1988 Carbon dating tests on the Shroud did not appear to take into consideration that something extraordinary happened at the Resurrection of Jesus Christ of Nazareth, which may have also released excessive radiation, and most likely the actual cause for how we see the photo-negative image on the Shroud now.

I also believe after much research that the Carbon Dating of the Shroud stated to be approximately 1325 A.D. is simply incorrect and easily explained by an incorrect interpretation of the cause of the additional radioactive molecules of Carbon (C-14) present in the Shroud, which was demonstrated by experiments on the Shroud.

In other words, rather than proving that the Shroud is dated somewhere about 1325 AD, rather it once again actually proves the Resurrection of Jesus Christ of Nazareth from over 2000 years ago.

The additional radioactive C-14 molecules proved and demonstrated by Dr. August Accetta, that the image on the Shroud was almost certainly caused by radiation.

Dr. Accetta actually injected into his own veins a solution of methylene diphosphate, containing radioactive technetium-99m, a radioisotope with a short half life. This caused the radiation from the technetium atoms to produce gamma rays, which were then able to be detected by the Gamma scanner Analysing Computer. So basically Dr. Accetta was able to produced an image on the Gamma scanner computer very similar to the image on the Shroud, but with not as much definition. It yielded some similar results but not the same as the Shroud. But clearly this demonstrated the Shroud was subjected to radiation, causing the photo-negative Image. There are many scientific tests that indicate that the Shroud is certainly from the First Century and now proving scientifically how the image on the Shroud could have probably been formed by Gamma rays. I suppose for example you might say in rather a similar way to the formation of X-rays that are used in Radiology departments of hospitals today. It only takes a moment to capture.

Then there is the "Hungarian Pray Manuscript" that was discovered and is known as "The Codex Pray" or "The Pray Codex," which was found in 1770 and clearly shows an old handwritten Hungarian text dating back to 1192 that illustrates that: Jesus was entirely naked with His arms on His pelvis, identical to The Shroud of Turin, That a woven fabric of a cloth existed showing a herringbone pattern, identical to the weaving pattern we see on The Shroud of Turin. There is also an illustration showing a piece of cloth that was identical to The Shroud of Turin. Along with an illustration showing the "poker holes" identical to the "poker holes" on The Shroud of Turin. In other words, the Hungarian Pray Manuscript serves as more evidence for the existence of the Shroud of Turin which pre-dates the radiocarbon 14 dating of The Shroud of Turin in 1988.

The best evidence for an incorrect date that has been published in peer reviewed scientific journals is that the sample chosen for dating was anomalous and not representative of the main body of the Shroud cloth itself. There is a lot of scientific evidence to support this claim.

4. Why should Christians care about the Shroud?

I feel I must point out that even without the Shroud of Turin, we, who have had a born again experience, have encountered a supernatural connection with the Lord of all creation. We don't need the Shroud to prove that Jesus is the Messiah and that the Bible is true, because we know from studying the Bible and personal experience it is true. Then again since we have the Shroud, why wouldn't we want to share the historical evidence to help the unbelievers and also encourage the believers with the Gospel truth? I mean it jolly well helps many people make the most important decision of their life when you present them with the evidence. Who in their right mind would ever turn away from the true Gospel once they encounter it? As every picture tells a story, to the born again, spirit-filled believer, the Shroud of Turin tells the story of God's amazing mercy, grace and love. Quite simply put, The Shroud of Turin proves the Resurrection of Jesus Christ of Nazareth and for that reason alone all Christians should deeply care about it. This world desperately needs to connect with the King of Kings and Lord of Lords, Messiah Jesus/Yashua. If it was the image of any other founder of some religion in this world, I dare say they would be broadcasting it everywhere and shouting about it from the rooftops. They would be going door-to-door to let everyone know. However, you can go to all the grave sites of every founder of religion in this world and their remains are still decomposing or now returned to dust, with the exception of the empty tomb of Jesus Christ of Nazareth because He is physically and eternally alive.

5. How do you think the image was made?

Personally I think the evidence is indicating that at the moment of the resurrection, the image on the Shroud was caused by the radiation given off by the body of Jesus within the Shroud. It appears to me that the image on the Shroud, which actually appears to almost be as if scorched (for lack of a better term) onto the fibers, was probably created by an extremely intense supernatural bombardment by subatomic particles, travelling at the speed of light. Because the Shroud appears to actually be like an X-ray radiograph, created at the moment the Resurrection of the Lord Jesus/ Yashua was taking place. We read about the glorious light of the Lord in the Bible so it seems highly probable to me that the Lord's radiant light caused this phenomena. Keeping in mind that Moses had to cover his face or "vail" his face because of the Shekinah Glory after being with the Lord.

Let me quote from Exodus 34:35, *"And the children of Israel saw the face of Moses, that the skin of Moses' face shone: and Moses put the vail upon his face again, until he went in to speak with him."*

Considering we don't know how long Moses had a face to face encounter with Papa God, however long or brief, it caused him to have to cover his face to the congregation of Israel as he glowed so intensely, perhaps as bright as the Sun. So, is it really so hard to now imagine that same Shekinah Glory of light happening during the Resurrection of Jesus of Nazareth? It seems rather obvious that the image was created by radiation.

As I have already shared briefly Dr. Accetta's experiment has shown that some sort of supernatural radioactive emission most likely caused the image on the Shroud to be visible to us, reminiscent of what we read about in the Transfiguration in Matthew 17:1-3: *"And after six days Jesus taketh Peter, James, and John his brother, and bringeth them up into an high mountain apart, And was transfigured before them: and his face did shine as the sun, and his raiment was white as the light. And, behold, there appeared unto them Moses and Elias talking with him."*

Anyone who has ever tried looking into the sun, knows you quickly need to look away. Did Jesus transcend the speed of light here and move into eternity when he was speaking with Moses and Elias? Albert Einstein showed us that space and time are essentially the same thing or rather it is 4th dimensional. It appears now there is actual physical evidence by examining the Shroud of Turin that greatly supports the position of the Zero/Infinity conflict, that we find between General Relativity and Quantum Mechanics. Obviously this was successfully dealt with by Christ's Resurrection. As time is continually travelling into the future, and the universe is continually expanding into something beyond. Is it possible to consider the entire universe was set up by the Lord to achieve this most awesome moment we celebrate over the Passover Resurrection holiday?

We read in 1 Peter 1: 20-21 *"Who verily was foreordained before the foundation of the world, but was manifest in these last times for you, Who by him do believe in God, that raised him up from the dead, and gave him glory; that your faith and hope might be in God."*

One of the things that is so amazing here is how all the known laws of science dealing with examination of the Shroud, find it conforms to no known law of physics. That there was apparently in the moment of Jesus Christ of Nazareth Resurrection a total lack of gravity without gravitational collapse. That essentially means there was no time and no space as we understand it presently.

We read in Isaiah 55:8-9 *"For my thoughts are not your thoughts, neither are your ways my ways, saith the LORD. For as the heavens are higher than the earth, so are my ways higher than your ways, and my thoughts than your thoughts."*

Nevertheless, we are to learn and practice thinking about things and seeing the world the way the Lord does by studying the Word of God in the Bible.

As you so elegantly call the "Guide Book to the Supernatural." We read in 1 Corinthians 2:16, *"For who hath known the mind of the Lord, that he may instruct him? But we have the mind of Christ."*

The supernatural image we see on the Shroud of Turin brings us what is termed a "true event horizon", meaning a moment when all laws of physics are drastically and dramatically altered and changed. We must accept and understand that all things are indeed possible with God, even that which seems impossible to us (Matthew 19:26).

6. The nail prints are not found in the area of the hand in what is depicted in most works of art, why is that?

This is another piece of compelling evidence, that the image of the body clearly shows that the arms had been nailed through both wrists, not the hands as so many Artist have ignorantly painted over time. If the nails went through the hands it would have caused the weight of the body to be torn through the fleshy part and come off the cross. The fact here that only four fingers are visible of both hands, suggests that there was injury to the Median nerve of both wrists that would cause the thumbs to turn inward like a claw. The Romans had soldiers who were assigned to do nothing but crucify those sentenced to death, and they were experts at locating this place between the wrist bones that has a small opening called, space of Destot, or Destot's point. Located between the first and second row of wrist bones (carpal bones) in the heel of the hand, we call the wrist. The nailing through Destot's point would hit the area of the median nerve, causing excruciating shocks of pain up the arms to the shoulders and neck, but without injury to major arterial trunks and without fracturing bones. Keep in mind the Bible prophesy says that not one of Christ's bones would be broken.

I seriously do not think any of us realize how much suffering the Lord Jesus went through to pay the penalty for the sins of this world. As well as keeping in mind that crucifixion was considered probably the most disgraceful and absolutely cruelest method of execution. It was most likely used only for revolutionaries and the worst of criminals.

7. How do you think the image was put on the cloth?

I would contend that the mechanism that left the image on the Shroud was certainly supernatural in its origins and therefore probably in some ways similar to what happened at the Transfiguration we read about in Matthew 17:1-8.

Many of the scientist who have been permitted to investigate the Shroud first hand appear to believe that the photo-negative image of Jesus Christ of Nazareth on the Shroud is fundamentally some sort of scorch type of markings. That at the moment of the Resurrection, supernatural radiation and light were emitted and scorched the surface fibrils of the linen cloth. This explanation of course accounts for the X-ray radiograph appearance of the Shroud. Now although it is believed there was fundamentally some sort of a nuclear type reaction which caused the emission of soft X-rays, the emission of light and subatomic particles would have obviously have had to been rather minimal. Considering the Shroud was not burnt up or damaged, other than the surface fibers of the linen cloths being affected. The Shroud is actually monochromatic as it is basically a single color, often described as yellowish-brown or sepia tone. The image of the crucified one is just a deeper shade of this same color.

The best way to view the image is from a distance because unlike a painting, the image almost disappears when you get up very close to it. Which begs the question:

How could an artist create such a work even today if they can not get close enough to work on it?

It appears to me that the linen was probably interacting at the moment of the Resurrection with a translational kinetic energy and the energy of this motion and the expansion, rapidly heating and vaporizing being the probably cause of the discolouration of the surface fibrils of the Shroud. Again this was supernaturally accomplished causing the image to be put on the Cloth.

Perhaps we see the image of the dead figure instead of being alive, simply because this world needed to understand and see this part of the Resurrection to understand and believe.

I had a minister friend who prayed for a blind girl at a church service who was born with only the whites of her eyes. He placed his hands on her face and closed his eyes to pray in faith for a miracle in Jesus name (probably more in obedience then in expectation and when he looked at her again after praying suddenly) she had pupils and was no longer blind. His first response was someone was playing a trick on him as he prayed and they somehow switched girls on him. There are simply now too many documented miracles today that have happened in Jesus/Yashua's name. This was the same response Jesus sent back to John the Baptist as he sat in prison entertaining a spirit of doubt.

Luke 7:22, *"Then Jesus answering said unto them, Go your way, and tell John what things ye have seen and heard; how that the blind see, the lame walk, the lepers are cleansed, the deaf hear, the dead are raised, to the poor the gospel is preached."*

Is it so surprising now to learn that the Shroud of Turin was dimensionally encoded in that moment, or that some radiation took place at the Resurrection that formed around the three dimensional body of Jesus Christ of Nazareth to be encoded onto a two dimensional linen Shroud?

Knowing that no one would even discover the technology to prove this until more than 2,000 years later. I praise the Lord for all the scientific and technological advances we have made so far. All things considered, the phenomenon of the Resurrection that caused the image of Jesus/Yashua, will forever be a supernatural event and that is simple a miracle.

As the great deception is played out in these last days that we read about in 2 Thessalonians Chapter 2 in the Bible, it is important to understand that no extraterrestrial or demon did this miracle.

Papa God fulfilled His prophesy in Resurrecting Jesus/Yashua and will continue to do exactly as He said He would because God says what He means and means what He says.

From careful examination, the image on the Shroud shows that the closer the cloth was in contact to the body of Jesus Christ of Nazareth, the more the image was highlighted in those areas. This means that the energy emitted at the moment of Christ's Resurrection probably was similar to what took place to His clothing at the Transfiguration. That there was some sort of radiation in ultraviolet, visible light and infrared spectrums. This somehow caused the photo negative image, giving it three dimensional properties, as the glorious light of God scorched onto the Shroud, with the intense light of the radiation and subatomic particles, bringing the emission of soft X-rays, that we now see complete with all the marks of the Scourging and the Crucifixion.

8. What would you say to the skeptic?

For all the "Doubting Thomas'" of the world, I am guessing you may possibly be sharing some trans-generational epigenetic inheritance with Thomas; in other words causing the changing of genetic codes to be prone to entertaining spirits of doubt and unbelief. Scripture teaches that rejection of truth is just as dangerous as entertaining a spirit of unbelief and faithlessness. The spirit of rejection tries to tell you that you need man's approval, and that places man ahead of the Lord. If Papa God made us in His image and likeness and then gave us His only begotten Son Jesus to make us whole, that surely is the ultimate act of acceptance.

We read in Mark 16:16-17 16 *"He that believeth and is baptized shall be saved; but he that believeth not shall be damned. And these signs shall follow them that believe; In my name shall they cast out devils; they shall speak with new tongues; They shall take up serpents; and if they drink any deadly thing, it shall not hurt them; they shall lay hands on the sick, and they shall recover."*

If you don't believe it, don't expect anything to happen, because without faith it is impossible to please the Lord.

We come to Christ just as we are in a fallen state, accepting His forgiveness and He gives us His Word that He will not cast us out.

Romans 8:31 *"What shall we then say to these things? If God be for us, who can be against us?"*

Keeping in mind that Papa God, Jesus Christ of Nazareth, and the Holy Spirit are certainly more powerful then any created being and every lie the devil has brought to you. That forever settles it for me, how about you?

Now I say all that because we need to also take into consideration that Artist Dame Piczek gives us some compelling insights for her work in particle physics, as she created a one-fourth size sculpture of the man in the Shroud. In her model as you view the image from the side, it appears as if the figure of the man is suspended in mid-air. In the science of thermodynamics, there is a term called entropy which is commonly associated with the amount of order, disorder, and/or chaos associated in the system of thermodynamics. With all that being said the image on the Shroud defies all previously accepted models of science.

Another amazing phenomena is that image on the Shroud appears as if it was created on the linen (like an artist canvas that was stretched quite taut) because there is no distortion on the image of the body. However we also know that there were folds and wrinkles as a bed covering would cause with someone lying underneath it, so again, it defies physics as we know it. The linen cloth also shows that where it was folded repeatedly the evidence strongly suggests it was folded and raised up mechanically in some sort of a Jack in the Box way, apparently this occurred in the early church services in Constantinople every Friday night. There is an account that describes this event in a rare book of memoirs by a French Crusader. Robert De Clari—who was an ordinary knight in the army—wrote about the many wonders to be seen in Constantinople as he and other visiting soldiers toured the city in 1203, Let me give you a quote:

"... another church called My Lady St. Mary of Blachernae, where there was the shroud [sydoines] in which Our Lord had been wrapped, which every Friday raised itself upright, so that one could see the figure of Our Lord on it ..." (Wilson 1991: 156).

The evidence here appears that the Church leaders in Constantinople mechanically raised up the Shroud (lest anyone think there was some sort of spiritualism going on here) as evidenced by the folds in the Linen.

It also seems rather plausible to me as you study to show yourself approved of the Lord, that the Apostle Paul and the early church congregations may have been aware of the image and mystery of the Lord's burial Shroud.

1 Corinthians 15:51 *"Behold, I shew you a mystery; We shall not all sleep, but we shall all be changed."*

May take on new meaning here. For we read in Acts 19:11, *"And God wrought special miracles by the hands of Paul. So that from his body were brought unto the sick handkerchiefs or aprons, and the diseases departed from them, and the evil spirits went out of them."*

You will find in Greek the word for "handkerchief" is "sudarium:" meaning a towel for wiping and cleaning the perspiration from the face, or for binding and covering the face of a corpse It is also called a napkin or sudarium.

Why didn't the Apostle Paul just lay on hands? What were these special miracles God performed through Paul? It is only conjecture here but is it possible Paul's handkerchiefs or aprons somehow touched the Shroud for these special healing miracles? Just as the women who touched the hem of Jesus garment? (Matthew 9:20)

New evidence continues to come in and supports the idea that the Shroud of Turin was displayed every Friday in ceremonies in Constantinople in the early church. Then the Shroud went missing for awhile in the 4th century as something happened during the crusades, which may have had the name Christian attached to it, which were certainly not handled as the Lord instructs His true disciples to behave. My point is, history is showing that the Shroud written about in Constantinople that had the image of Christ on it, is most likely the same Shroud of Turin. We read in 2 Corinthians 4:6, *"For God, who commanded the light to shine out of darkness, hath shined in our hearts, to give the light of the knowledge of the glory of God in the face of Jesus Christ."*

The light of the Gospel shining into our darkened hearts and thought life is like the bursting forth of the sun in darkness. Hallelujah.

9. Are you familiar with the so-called restoration done on the Shroud and how it destroyed any forensic evidence for future generations? Please give us your thoughts on this.

Back in 2002 it is now known that the Shroud of Turin was subjected to some radical restoration done in the name of intervention. The reason given was supposedly to rid the Shroud of carbon dust and charred material said to pose a serious threat to the image. It was done in secret at the time, because vacuuming was permitted to be done to both sides, and other remedial measures were taken to supposedly optimize the appearance of the Shroud. I should think there would have been quite a lot of opposition from researchers if this act was done in the light of day. This, of course, has resulted in important scientific data being forever lost and for more future opportunities with advancement of sophisticated testing and sampling to be done. It is obvious now that long-term this has had rather a negative impact. This so called "intervention" is said to have been substantial; and clearly the premise that the image on the Shroud was somehow threatened has been shown to be a false claim. Now why would anyone want to destroy the evidence of the Shroud and put out so much misinformation and try to persuade the public that it is nothing more then a clever medieval forgery? I recall reading some article years ago in a popular publication where they were claiming proof that the Shroud was a fake and not the burial cloth of Christ, just as evolutionist think they have proof of evolution when in fact all they have is faulty theories and not a shred of evidence. So I wrote to the editor of this particular popular magazine and presented the actual facts. The editor wrote me back and stated it was their position to go with the popular opinion. Never mind the truth, and that is the way of the world sadly. I pray we have brought you the Gospel truth here.

10. Your Closing Thoughts?

May I share this, as we read in John 20:25-31: [25]*"The other disciples therefore said unto him, We have seen the LORD. But he said unto them, Except I shall see in his hands the print of the nails, and put my finger into the print of the nails, and thrust my hand into his side, I will not believe.* [26]*And after eight days again his disciples were within, and Thomas with them: then came Jesus, the doors being shut, and stood in the midst, and said, Peace be unto you. ²⁷Then saith he to Thomas, Reach hither thy finger, and behold my hands; and reach hither thy hand, and thrust it into my side: and be not faithless, but believing.*

And then jumping down to: verse 28:

²⁸And Thomas answered and said unto him, My LORD and my God. ²⁹Jesus saith unto him, Thomas, because thou hast seen me, thou hast believed: blessed are they that have not seen, and yet have believed. ³⁰And many other signs truly did Jesus in the presence of his disciples, which are not written in this book: ³¹But these are written, that ye might believe that Jesus is the Christ, the Son of God; and that believing ye might have life through his name."

What about today with the people who refuse to believe the whole Gospel and want some physical evidence? Or those who call themselves Christians but continue to sin like heathens thinking that modern message of God's grace on steroids covers them in their rebellion and disobedience to the Word of God. As the Lord Jesus said a number of times, "have you not read?" May I ask that today? Have you not read Romans 6:1? *"What shall we say then? Shall we continue in sin, that grace may abound? God forbid. How shall we, that are dead to sin, live any longer therein?"*

The other side of this understanding is what sin actually is. We often think of sin as cheating, lying and stealing and that sort of thing. What about entertaining the spirit of unforgiveness and bitterness, envy and jealousy and anger which releases toxic chemicals into your body and hinders your walking in the blessings of Abraham that the Lord wants you to have? Or entertaining the spirit of fear in your thought life? Along with its modern words of terminology we call anxiety and stress. The Bible says fear is a sin because Papa God did not give it to you. May I give you a Scripture?

Romans 14:23, *"And he that doubteth is damned if he eat, because he eateth not of faith: for whatsoever is not of faith is sin."*

The Lord gave us a spirit of power, love and a sound mind as found in 2 Timothy 1:7, *"For God hath not given us the spirit of fear; but of power, and of love, and of a sound mind."*

The Lord also gave us an amazing supernatural holographic type picture which has preserved the moment of Jesus Christ of Nazareth's glorious resurrection. It is the evidence recorded on the burial cloth that wrapped his entire body.

It is available to the world and we ought to know about it.

Most Christians I speak with do not have a clue about this physical evidence. The Shroud of Turin is a very detailed and graphic picture of the death of Papa God's only begotten Son, Jesus/Yashua by crucifixion. It is clearly a detailed account of the suffering and pain the Lord Jesus endured on that Roman Cross to provide a way for the salvation of every person who will accept his amazing mercy, grace and love and continue in His Word. In fact Jesus said in Matthew 16:24, *"Then said Jesus unto his disciples, If any man will come after me, let him deny himself, and take up his cross, and follow me."*

If Papa God forgives us we must forgive ourselves and everyone else from our hearts, according to what the Lord instructed us to do in places like Matthew 18. That means you tear up that record of wrongs you held against others and even yourself. It is not for us to ever say we can not forgive as Christians if Jesus forgave whilst suffering excruciating pain in our place on that cross and led that thief into salvation next to Him. What are we to do then? Papa God is the ultimate judge, not us. Besides, Jesus went to the cross so we could be blessed. So we could have a more abundant life. So we won't struggle in our families and careers and suffer health problems.

The Bible says the curse cannot come without a reason. Proverbs 26:2, *"As the bird by wandering, as the swallow by flying, so the curse causeless shall not come."*

If we recognize some place in our life where we are not prospering physically, emotionally, spiritually, financially or in our relationship, then its time to take spiritual inventory and go before the Lord's throne of mercy, grace and love. 1st John 1:9-10,*"If we confess our sins, he is faithful and just to forgive us our sins, and to cleanse us from all unrighteousness. If we say that we have not sinned, we make him a liar, and his word is not in us."*

If we confess our sins to Him and He says He forgives us, we dare not deny any of God's power to do so. Who are we to condemn ourselves or anyone else for that matter, when the Judge of all the earth acquits us?

The Lord tells us over and over again once we repent and confess our sins, *"be of good cheer; thy sins be forgiven thee"* (Matthew 9:2).

I should think getting healed and delivered by the Lord Jesus will make you cheerful and eternally grateful. If Jesus redeemed us from the curse of the law, then why should we be suffering with any lack now in our life's? According to Galatians 3:13,*"Christ hath redeemed us from the curse of the law, being made a curse for us: for it is written, Cursed is every one that hangeth on a tree:14 That the blessing of Abraham might come on the Gentiles through Jesus Christ; that we might receive the promise of the Spirit through faith."*

Because the devil has worked hard to try and take people away from the Gospel truth and try and fill their hearts and imaginations with ungodly toxic thinking, this has caused strife and division through the spirit of fear and witchcraft and manipulations. However, the Lord will always outmaneuver anything the devil does, Hallelujah. The Lord gave us clear instructions about blessings and curses in places like Deuteronomy 28 that we might be blessed and achieve our potential as a child of God by using our mouth to speak and bring forth blessings.

Mark 11:24, *"Therefore I say unto you, What things soever ye desire, when ye pray, believe that ye receive them, and ye shall have them."*

If you need help to believe and overcome entertaining the spirit of doubt and unbelief, let us consider the Lord Jesus's glorious resurrection and the extraordinary evidence He presented us in the Shroud of Turin.

Proof of Virgin Birth

I had a physician friend who told me back in 2001 that if scientists could ever prove the DNA samples that only showed the parent's gene, that should settle the Shroud debate. Even with all the modern communication technologies we have available today certain important information still travels slowly, lest anyone forget we are in a multidimensional spiritual battle each day.

Ephesians 2:2, *"Wherein in time past ye walked according to the course of this world, according to the prince of the power of the air, the spirit that now worketh in the children of disobedience:"*

If the Gospels' account of the virgin birth are indeed true, then Jesus' DNA makeup would have no Y chromosome because He did not have a human father after all, but instead would have two X chromosomes.

I just wanted to share with you one last thing to take away from this book and that is scientist have indeed confirmed this by taking DNA samples from the Sudarium of Oviedo, which is the handkerchief that covered Jesus face and DNA samples from the Shroud of Turin. Keeping in mind that since Jesus was born fully male, that would mean He must have the SRY gene. However, researchers found that the SRY gene, instead of being in the Y chromosome, was inserted into a location where it is not normally found as it was discovered inside one of the two X chromosomes imparted from Mary, His mother.

In January of 1995, a team of Italian researchers led by Professor Marcello Canale of the Institute of Legal Medicine in Genoa—which also included several researchers who had helped invent the standard DNA test for gender—were able to conduct a DNA analysis of the blood on the Shroud of Turin and on the Oviedo Cloth (also called the Sudarium of Oviedo).

Yes, my friends, scientists discovered that the X chromosome is present, but there is no evidence of a Y chromosome. This is of course to be the expected signature of a virgin birth!!! That makes me very happy, because there is physical proof for the skeptics and unbelievers to believe that what the Lord Jesus said and did is 100% true!!!

Now unless there was another virgin who gave birth to a man who was crucified wearing a crown of thorns and pierced in his side, and was nailed through his hands and feet with over 120 scourge marks who supernaturally left his image on his burial cloth, I think the evidence speaks for itself.

If you understand the significance of the Passover/Resurrection, you automatically understand what Jesus/Yeshua of Nazareth did for you. Then how can you not worship and celebrate the Lord in the fullness of His glory and His blessings for you? The Lord said in Luke 21:15 *"For I will give you a mouth and wisdom, which all your adversaries shall not be able to gainsay nor resist."*

I say hallelujah! Because "All", things are possible with God!

I pray blessings on you always in Jesus Christ of Nazareth/Messiah Yashua's all Powerful Name.

Thanks for asking such wonderful questions and letting me share all this with your readers L. A.

Caspar McCloud

This concludes the interview.

FINAL THOUGHTS

My encouragement for you is to love God, love people and minister healing and miracles in Jesus (Yeshua's) all powerful Name!

The Lord Jesus Christ of Nazareth is forever alive.

Malachi 3:6, *"For I am the LORD, I change not; therefore ye sons of Jacob are not consumed."*

Hebrews 13:8, *"Jesus Christ the same yesterday, and to day, and for ever."*

My friend L. A. Marzulli has called the Shroud of Turin, "Jesus' Calling Card" and I think this is a card that needs to be presented now more then ever to this fallen world. It appears to me there are only two kinds of people in this world, those who are born again and those who need to be born again.

After participating with Russ Breault's "Shroud Encounter" numerous times, he has impressed upon me and his audiences the significance of the compelling message we are able to read from the recorded image on the Shroud. The words that strongly indicate a great unknown price was paid. Breault often ends his marvelous presentation by sharing how the words " Relic"—"Artifact"—"Symbol"—"Mystery" are often the sort of words most people use to describe what the Shroud is. However they are all rather inadequate words to describe its propose. We feel the words "BOUGHT"—"PURCHASE"—"REDEEMED"—"RANSOM" helps convey the divine purpose and this concept needs to be seriously considered.

Because you and I were bought with a price, you should live a life now that is glorifying to God in your body and in all you do.

1 Corinthians 6:19-20, *[19]"What? know ye not that your body is the temple of the Holy Ghost which is in you, which ye have of God, and ye are not your own? [20]For ye are*

bought with a price: therefore glorify God in your body, and in your spirit, which are God's."

We were purchased with the blood of God.

Acts 20:28, *"Take heed therefore unto yourselves, and to all the flock, over the which the Holy Ghost hath made you overseers, to feed the church of God, which he hath purchased with his own blood."*

After we confess we have sinned and fallen short of the glory of God, we are able to be redeemed:

1 Peter 1:18 *[18]"Forasmuch as ye know that ye were not redeemed with corruptible things, as silver and gold, from your vain conversation received by tradition from your fathers; [19]But with the precious blood of Christ, as of a lamb without blemish and without spot:"*

Christ gave himself as a ransom for you and I.

Mark 10:45 *"For even the Son of man came not to be ministered unto, but to minister, and to give his life a ransom for many."*

Breault shares how when you go to purchase anything the cashier always provides you with a receipt. What is a receipt but a proof of purchase with an itemized list of what you paid for? This is indeed the receipt we have as true believers been given. Most people take receipts of value and keep them somewhere safe. How much more shall we keep such a receipt now in our hearts?

I tell you the truth; there is an invisible spiritual battle going on every day. Most of the world is walking about wounded with broken hearts and Jesus came to mend broken hearts. Whenever we meet as the church there are many issues to address as churches are not designed to minister to perfect people. Papa God designed His church to be like a clinic and to minister to the sick and broken-hearted so that they can be healed and restored and blessed beyond what they can even imagine.

We read in Galatians 6:1-2, *¹"Brethren, if a man be overtaken in a fault, ye which are spiritual, restore such an one in the spirit of meekness; considering thyself, lest thou also be tempted. ²Bear ye one another's burdens, and so fulfil the law of Christ."*

In other words, all those Christians who are a bit stronger and mature in the Word are to help those who are feeling weak and struggling. All those who have been forgiven of Christ must forgive all others. All those who have been supernaturally healed by Christ be used of the Lord to help heal others through the gifts of the Holy Spirit. All those who have been restored and comforted by Christ help restore and comfort others.

The devil always hurts and kicks people when they are down and discouraged; however, it is the body of Christ, His Church that needs to minister mercy, grace, love and understanding and help them recover. Let us pray that we decrease so the Lord Jesus Christ of Nazareth increases in us and that we are always a blessings to others. In fact the Lord Jesus instructs his followers to share the Gospel, heal the sick and cast out demons in the authority of His Almighty Name.

John 14:12, *"Verily, verily, I say unto you, He that believeth on me, the works that I do shall he do also; and greater works than these shall he do; because I go unto my Father."*

Seriously, if every believer would simply just do as the Lord has commended I believe we certainly be seeing a greater supernatural move within His church to fulfill these greater works in His almighty name.

All those wounds that Jesus suffered that we are able to observe on the Shroud of Turin paid for your healing for today.

Exodus 15:26....*"for I am the LORD that healeth thee.."*

1 Peter 2:24, *"...by whose stripes ye were healed."*

Isaiah 53:4, *"Surely he hath borne our griefs, and carried our sorrows: yet we did esteem him stricken, smitten of God, and afflicted."*

Your complete healing was already paid for by the precious Blood of Jesus!

The Lord Jesus has given us authority over all demonic spirits as stated in Luke 10:19, *"Behold, I give unto you power to tread on serpents and scorpions, and over all the power of the enemy: and nothing shall by any means hurt you."*

The thing is that along with such awesome authority also comes responsibility. Behind most sickness and diseases there is a spiritual dynamic that is often overlooked that began in someone's thought life. The science of epigenetics is now even showing that 80% to 98% of all sickness and diseases begin in the mind. We read many times how the Lord Jesus cast an evil spirit out then healed the person. For example, Matthew 10:1, *"And when he had called unto him his twelve disciples, he gave them power against unclean spirits, to cast them out, and to heal all manner of sickness and all manner of disease."*

In other words, we were not given authority over demonic spirits and told to cast them out for no good reason! When we pray over a person who is being tormented and ask the Lord to remove it, as the modern church has taught, we are basically asking Jesus to do something that in fact He clearly told us to do:

Matthew 10:7, *"And as ye go, preach, saying, The kingdom of heaven is at hand. 8 Heal the sick, cleanse the lepers, raise the dead, cast out devils: freely ye have received, freely give."*

Mark 11:24, *"Therefore I say unto you, What things soever ye desire, when ye pray, believe that ye receive them, and ye shall have them."*

Mark 16:14-20, *¹⁴"Afterward he appeared unto the eleven as they sat at meat, and upbraided them with their unbelief and hardness of heart, because they believed not them which had seen him after he was risen. ¹⁵And he said unto them, Go ye into all the world, and preach the gospel to every creature. ¹⁶He that believeth and is baptized shall be saved; but he that believeth not shall be damned. ¹⁷And these signs shall follow them that believe; In my name shall they cast out devils; they shall speak with new tongues; ¹⁸they shall take up serpents; and if they drink any deadly thing, it shall not hurt them; they shall lay hands on the sick, and they shall recover. ¹⁹So then after the Lord had spoken unto them, he was received up into heaven, and sat on the right hand of God. ²⁰And they went forth, and preached every where, the Lord working with them, and confirming the word with signs following. Amen."*

All things are possible with God! I pray the Lord's supernatural peace, healing, provision and protection cover you always with oceans of agape love in the almighty name of Jesus/Yeshua!

Pastor Caspar McCloud

PICTURES

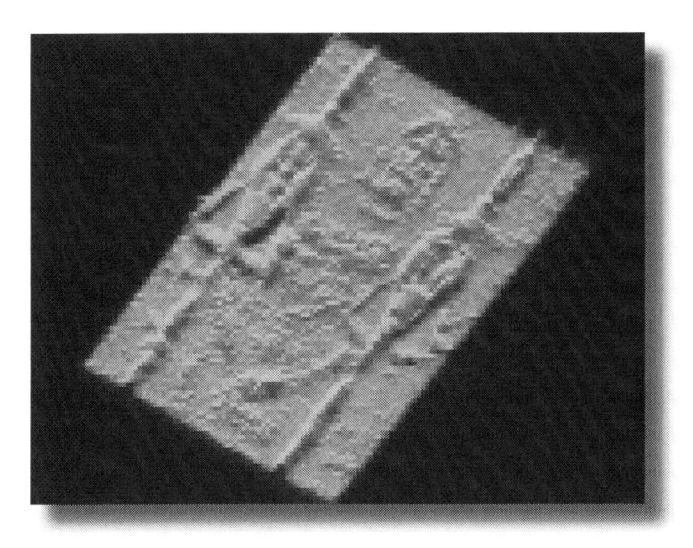

3/4 View of the Ventral Image of the Shroud of Turin taken from the screen of a VP-8 Image Analyzer, the device used by the STURP team in 1978.

© 1997 Barrie M. Schwortz Collection, STERA, Inc. All Rights Reserved

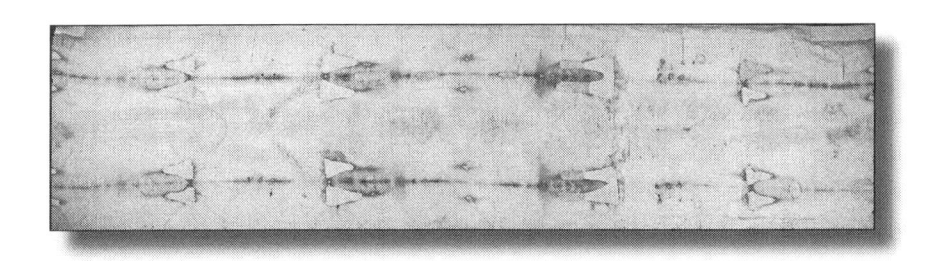

The full Shroud of Turin in natural color as photographed during the 1978 scientific examination.

© 1978 Barrie M. Schwortz Collection, STERA, Inc. All Rights Reserved

Contrast Enhanced Shroud of Turin Facial Image as it appears on a photographic negative

© 1978 Barrie M. Schwortz Collection, STERA, Inc. All Rights Reserved.

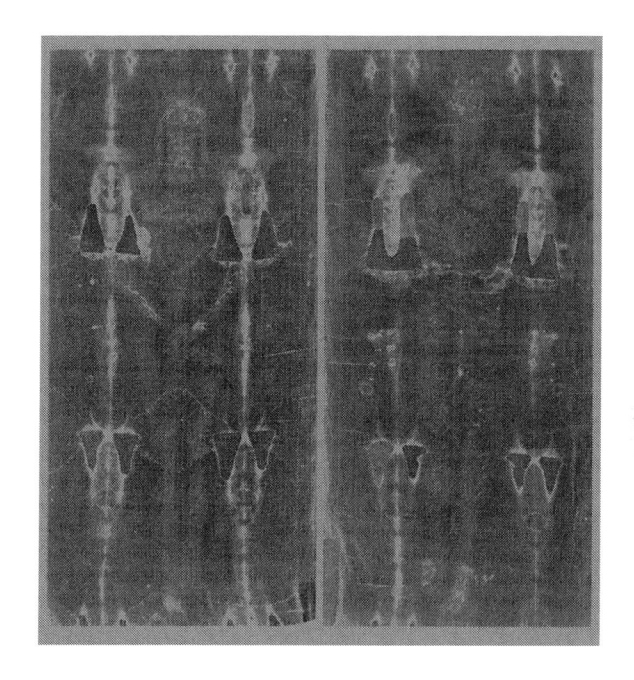

The side by side ventral and dorsal images of the Shroud of Turin as they appear on a photographic negative.

© 1978 Barrie M. Schwortz Collection, STERA, Inc. All Rights Reserved

Barrie Schwortz (right), STURP Documenting Photographer, makes large format photographs of the Shroud during the 1978 scientific examination of the cloth.

© 1978 Barrie M. Schwortz Collection, STERA, Inc. All Rights Reserved

STURP team members (left to right) Tom D'Muhula, Roger Gilbert and Bob Dinegar (at foot of table) take a first look at the Shroud while it is still fastened to the white wooden board upon which it had been publicly displayed. The STURP examination table is visible in background with most of its removable panels covered with gold foil mylar.

© 1978 Barrie M. Schwortz Collection, STERA, Inc. All Rights Reserved

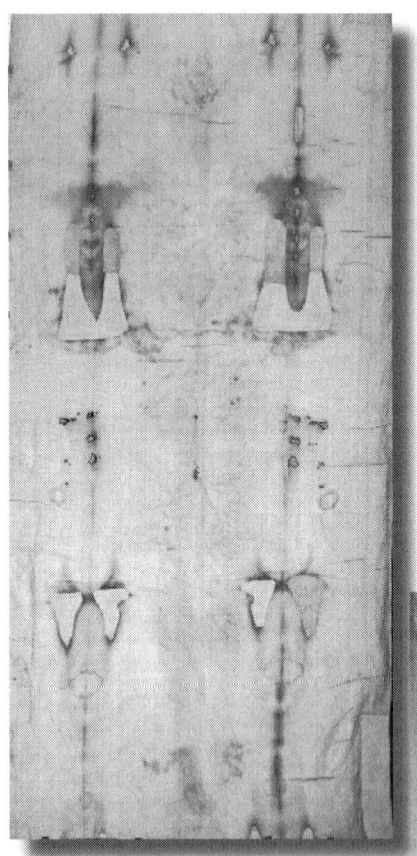

The Dorsal (Back) view of the Shroud of Turin as it appears in natural light.

© 1978 Barrie M. Schwortz Collection, STERA, Inc. All Rights Reserved

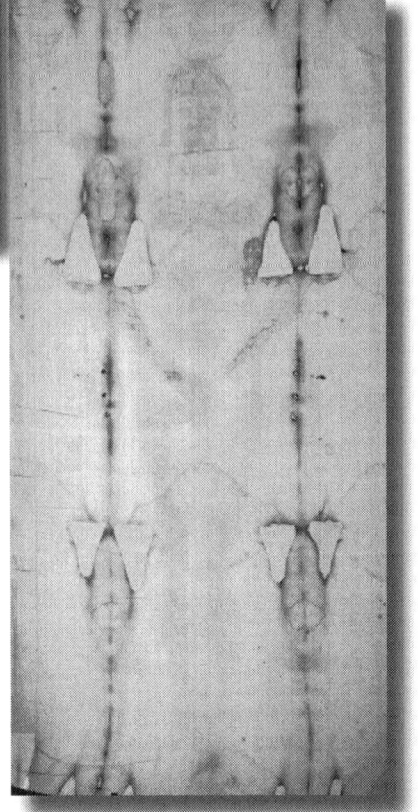

The Ventral (Frontal) view of the Shroud of Turin as it appears in natural light.

© 1978 Barrie M. Schwortz Collection, STERA, Inc. All Rights Reserved

On the Shroud scientific research has determined

The Dimensions of the Shroud Linen Cloth is measured length of 14.25 feet by width of 3.58 feet

1. Blood by the feet
2. Hands showing no thumbs
3. Nail wound in the wrist
4. Blood on the arms
5. Side wound
6. Face and hair
7. Blood on forehead
8. Punctures from crown of thorns
9. Scourge marks from neck to ankles
10. Blood from side wound
11. Right leg elevated above left
12. Left foot with two exits wounds
13. Right heal
14. Water stains that occurred when fire in 1532 was doused
15. Parallel lines on either side of image are scorch marks
16. Seams runs entire length of cloth
17. Burns and patches from 1532 fire
18. L- shaped burn holes from earlier burn incident
19. Section cut out in 1500's

Ron London (left) and William Mottern, STURP Radiology team members, set up their equipment in front of the Shroud of Turin.

© 1978 Barrie M. Schwortz Collection, STERA, Inc. All Rights Reserved

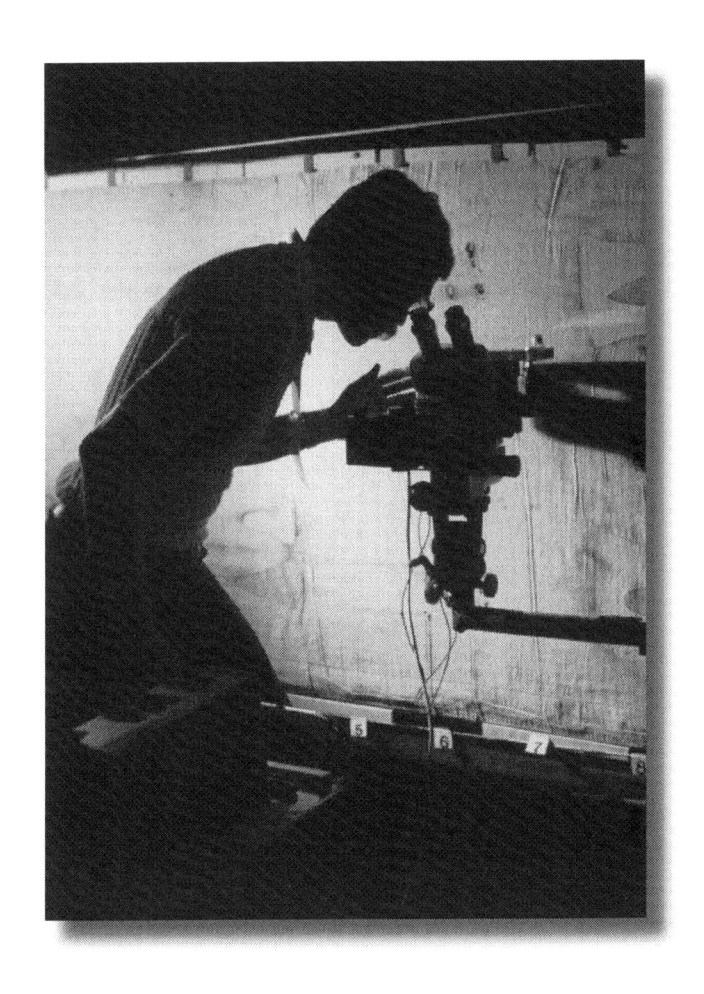

Researcher Mark Evans examines the Shroud of Turin with a special photographic microscope during the 1978 scientific examination of the cloth.

© 1978 Barrie M. Schwortz Collection, STERA, Inc.
All Rights Reserved.

Professor Giovanni Riggi (foreground) separates the Shroud of Turin from its backing cloth with a special instrument designed to hold the cloths apart, as his assistant, Gabriele Porratti, looks on. Both were members of the international team that examined the Shroud for 120 hours in 1978.

© 1978 Barrie M. Schwortz Collection, STERA, Inc. All Rights Reserved

From left to right:
John Jackson, Rebecca Jackson, Russ Breault, Caspar McCloud and Barrie Schwortz

Caspar and Russ enjoying a meal and fellowship after a conference with members of the original Shroud team.

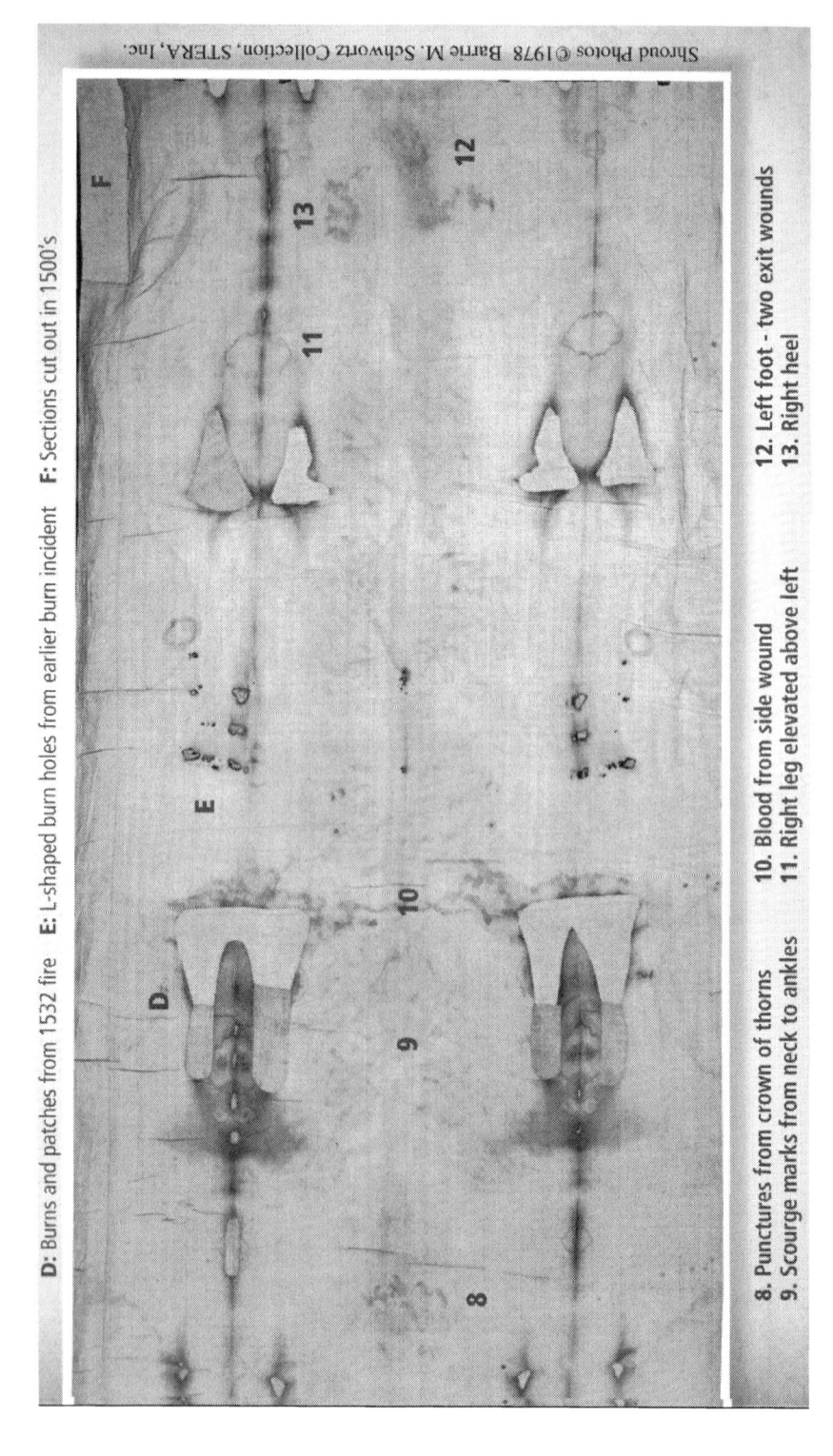

D: Burns and patches from 1532 fire **E:** L-shaped burn holes from earlier burn incident **F:** Sections cut out in 1500's

8. Punctures from crown of thorns   10. Blood from side wound   12. Left foot - two exit wounds
9. Scourge marks from neck to ankles 11. Right leg elevated above left   13. Right heel

Shroud Photos ©1978 Barrie M. Schwortz Collection, STERA, Inc.

FULL LINEN CLOTH DIMENSIONS: length 14.25 ft. x width 3.58 ft.
A: Water stains occurred when fire was doused **B:** Parallel lines on either side of image are scorch marks **C:** Seam runs entire length of cloth

1. Blood by feet
2. Hands–no thumbs
3. Nail wound in wrist
4. Blood on arms
5. Side wound
6. Face and hair
7. Blood on forehead

SALVATION PRAYER

If you have not yet received the most awesome gift of God, Salvation through Jesus Christ, then pray this simple prayer and start a new life in Christ:

"Dear God Almighty, my Heavenly Father, I come to You now in the all powerful name of Jesus Christ of Nazareth, Messiah Yeshua. I freely confess and admit that I have not been living right before You, and I recognise that I truly need and want to be right with You forever more. I ask You Lord to please forgive me now of all my sins and fill me with your Holy Spirit. Your Holy Bible says that if I confess with my mouth that "Jesus is Lord," and believe in my heart that God raised Him from the dead, I will be saved (Romans 10:9). So Lord I believe with all my heart and I confess with my mouth that Jesus is now the Lord and Saviour of my life and want to live a life that is glorifying to Christ.

Because I truly believe that Jesus died in my place as payment for all my sins, and that He rose again defeating the power of sin and death that I might be saved and born again. Because you are so merciful to forgiven me now and wash me clean from all unrighteousness, I choose to also forgive from my heart all those who have done wrong to me, including being able now to forgive myself.

Thank You for saving me, I am so eternally grateful for what you have done for me!
I pray this in Jesus' name. Amen."

If you prayed this prayer for the first time, we would love to know about it.

Please send me an e-mail or share your testimony at pastorcaspar@gmail.com

or

www.theupperroomfellowship.org

MORE BOOKS AND TEACHINGS

For more information on healing and miracles read:

- Revised book: *Nothing Is Impossible* by Caspar McCloud
- *What Was I Thinking?* co authored with Linda Lange of Life Application Ministries and Caspar McCloud
- *Exposing the Spirit of Self-Pity by Caspar McCloud*
- *The Evidence of the Shroud Speaks for Itself* by Simon Brown and Caspar McCloud

  My co author Simon Brown actually took measurements of the sepulchre where the body of Jesus was laid in the Garden Tomb (which is of course connected to the Shroud) and he also discovered the great stone that was rolled away. The sepulchre measures just over 6 foot long and the image on the Shroud is 5 foot 11 inches.

  The great Stone only fits in the channel hewn out of the stone of the Garden Tomb. You will find this and the latest research and more evidence in our new book, "The Evidence of the Shroud Speaks for Itself."

Books also available at:

- www.realdiscoveries.org
- www.theupperroomfellowship.org
- www.Amazon.com
- www.jesus-loves-you.info

CONTACT US

Pastor Caspar McCloud

Upper Room Fellowship
1901 Batesville Road, Canton GA 30115
(770) 380-2749

pastorcaspar@gmail.com
www.theupperroomfellowship.org
Non-Profit 501c3

Printed in Great
Britain
by Amazon